Above Palm Canyon
and Other Places
in the Mind

Poems

Per K. Brask

FICTIVE
PRESS

FICTIVE PRESS

(a division of 2815699 Canada Inc.)

Copyright © 2013 by Per K. Brask.

First published in 2013 by FICTIVE PRESS, a division of 2815699 Canada Inc., British Columbia, Canada.

Distributed in Canada and worldwide by FICTIVE PRESS.

fictivepress.com

"FICTIVE PRESS" is a trademark of 2815699 Canada Inc.

The following poems in this collection were previously published in *Consciousness, Literature and the Arts* Vol. 10, No. 2, in 2009:

"I-94 West," "Thank the Gods for Missoula," "West of Spokane," "Little Girl Racing," Crowsnest Pass," and "Close to Home."

"A Friend from Way Back When," was previously published in *Consciousness, Literature and the Arts* Vol. 13, No. 1, in 2012.

Library and Archives Canada Cataloguing in Publication

Brask, Per K., 1952-

Above Palm Canyon and other places in the mind / Per K. Brask.

Poems.

Issued also in electronic formats.

ISBN 978-0-9879170-9-6

I. Title.

PS8553.R296A66 2013   C811'.54   C2013-900034-8

Back cover photo of Per K. Brask by Bonnie Brask, Bonnie Jean Photography

Cover photo by Per K. Brask

Cover design by FICTIVE PRESS

For Carol, of course

Good road trips not only get you to a destination, good road trips allow you time for meditation and observation; they make you ready for arrival. Though you may just be driving through Spokane, WA, with a stop at Starbucks, or stretching your legs walking along the river, you do sense that things are done differently there; they even drive slightly more recklessly on the freeway than they did in Missoula, MT. (Which is jarring when you pass a casket-maker's truck.)

For my wife, Carol, and me, our preferred destinations are the Sonoran Desert around Palm Springs, CA, where we both find a unique kind of beauty and spiritual alignment; and Portland, OR, where we visit grandchildren and their parents and lots of excitement takes place.

The poems in this collection are meditations on the journey and the arrival.

Per K. Brask

CONTENTS

ON THE ROAD

I-94 WEST

Valley City looks oh so pretty
when we arrive from the east
on the I-94. The mist rises
off the still drenched prairie.
Hugh Fraser's soothing voice
puts you into an alpha state
from time to time. Luckily
I'm driving. He announces
"Murder," in our mystery.

In Dickinson we find the Badlands
Coffee Bar nicely disguised in an old church.
We sit in pews flecked with light spilling through
stained glass and study the admonition
that "unattended children will be given
an espresso and a puppy."

The badlands are filled with such mysteries;
the occasional bison protected by Theodore Roosevelt
and on the side of the road occasional carcasses of deer
protected by no one.

THANK THE GODS FOR MISSOULA

The structure of a day can turn out
much like a road trip in Montana;
the hotel in Billings has a great breakfast
and you got up in plenty of time to predict
an easy ride to Spokane, WA.
A couple of hours later and after a stop
to purchase roadside earrings
the GPS guides you through the clean brick of old Bozeman
to a roastery. But it's early and lunch can wait till Butte
– this coffee is treat enough – except Butte is a dump
where lactose-free cheese can't be had for money
and an hour is wasted in a depressed mining burg
after which not even the sight of gliding hawks can lift your soul.

Thank the gods for Missoula and the Double Tree's foresight
to put a restaurant patio right next to the swelled Clark's Fork
where sun and salmon redeem the day before the last push.

WEST OF SPOKANE

Somewhere just west of Spokane
with the sun at our backs
we are advised to please drive safely
because heaven can wait
by a truck from Batesville Casket Co.

Then we head south to Pasco
and the nuclear power station there
thinking about all the ways
a person can find trouble.

We choose our pancakes at the IHOP
for their harvest grain healthy goodness,
after which the Columbia River Gorge
recalculates our destinies
into a spectacular reprieve.

LITTLE GIRL RACING

Life seems to become most vibrant in the margins
as when I take a picture of my son going to the podium
to be hooded.
It is the boy he was riding on my shoulders I see
not the lawyer he is now.
It is his daughter having had it with sitting
now wanting to play, who carries the weight of today
not the handshake he receives from Bob Bennett
and it is my father's unstoppable sneezing, his irritation
at its interference
that makes me proud to be part of the chain that's led us
to this day the purpose of which years from now may be revealed
by a little girl eager to race up the stairs and out into the sun
in the parking lot.

CROWSNEST PASS

In a Tim's in the Crowsnest Pass
three teachers are gathered
to talk about kids – their own
and those they teach.
They talk about testosterone
while I gaze up at mountain peaks
and think about what the hell it was
apart from coal
that made this pass so important in history:
something about the CPR
and the transportation of grain in the 1890s
or something about rumrunners later on
and much earlier wasn't there something
about the Crow and the Blackfoot?
I kinda want to ask the teachers
but I get a steeped tea instead.

CLOSE TO HOME

Apart from our waitress at Earl's there's nothing
very pretty about Regina, and she has bad breath.
Driving on the prairie requires a really good audio book
so we pick up Philip Roth's *Everyman* at Chapters for the last leg.
It's about mortality, the end of things, Death with a capital D
and it somehow suits our mood
and very importantly it fits the time of our ride.
The sex scenes are disappointingly unnecessary,
but that comes with the territory
so we overlook them, accept them as a flat stretch of story
that we just have to get through to get to the good stuff.

IN BETWEEN

MY MIND'S RIDGEPOLE

My mind's ridgepole is sagging
for no single good reason. The reasons are legion.
Like the saddled-backed house down the street across from the church
it's burdened with proximity to over-much belief,
unable to produce enough unbelief to counteract this pressure.
It's now close to bursting in on itself, imploding like a dying star,
a black hole in a firmament that's no longer there when the light vanishes.

The centre is holding too fast.
A gravitational field is sundering our world; we are deluged by belief.
Ends are torn from their grasp. There are but moments left
to learn the stabilizing force of unrighteousness and indulge ourselves
on a raft of mutual benefit – where no one can be all right.

LODESTAR

Though of Polaris there may only be one
many lodestars are scattered through a life, a moment even.
Nations seem to have theirs, as Israel's is survival
and the US's is to have and to hold – everything.
It depends on who and what you follow and who and what you lead.
Days can go by where merely getting from one to the next is enough.
Then suddenly a call, shopping lists drop and become contentious,
a new order of the real asserts itself. What will you conserve, what
reform?

The firmament changes shape like a kaleidoscope; new colours light up
and you know where you're going because you're already on your way.
The journey itself some tell you is the aim. It's not about the destination.
But if your lodestar assures success and adoration you'll have no journey
at all.

PUSHBACK

This is meant as pushback, a means of getting rid of excess.
The weight it struggles against is mainly from expectations and fantasies.
It wants to stand on its own, in so far as anyone one can.
All is webbed in language, in biology, and the rest
but we can stand against, we can say enough, we can say remember.
The future depends on it.

The roots of the felled tree by the fence are sprouting new shoots.
It's starting afresh after growing itself to death;
not as resurrection but as continuance in a new lighter path.
Perhaps the old tree has already become this sheet of paper
still pushing back?

WITHDRAWAL

Withdrawal is such a bitter-sweet scent to wear.
Its anonymous mask gives a privileged view of the fury.
And as much as you may be tempted to engage,
to get your whole self into the scrimmage,
feeling alive because of the cuts (received and delivered)
it may well be that you should stay concealed
until you know how best to plunge.
Not every battle is valuable.

Winter must come every year
as spring surely must, too.
Darkness always lasts too long but it takes time
to refine what we want when the light returns.

WALKING

We've walked and talked in the Sonoran desert and in the streets of NYC
our path has taken us through Copenhagen and LA.

(But mostly we've talked up and down Wellington Crescent and through
the Park).

In some places we stomped our feet to feel the earth's response,
in others we had to tread carefully for fear of what might bite us.

It's clear that we like our desert talks the best, they've been means of joy,
but those morning walks along the Assiniboine have been indispensable.

(Could that be because of the trees?)

LEAVE ME ALONE

Once partying, socializing, schmoozing
came (too) easily, like breathing.
Now it's a chore, like snow removal or DIY assembly,
causing a lot of sweat and swearing.

Yet things only happen when people come together.

On my cousin's farm a beer and a chat with neighbours motivated
the disappearance of huge boulders and the mending of fences.

Life truly is with others
but I struggle with, Leave me alone
please.

CHANGE

Nature has it right, of course (that's nature's job):
change is the only constant.
It isn't only that everything has its season.
It's that nothing is ever settled.

The story going on in my mind is as solid
as clouds drifting across the sky.
Change, all is change, even radical change
occurring at relative speeds throughout creation.

What was will never be again
and all that we consider enduring, like the bible(s), like Shakespeare,
endures because we keep changing our minds about them,
see in them something new, something changed.

As soon as we try to affix something to forever
it dies and we die (more quickly) with it.

HAPPY FAMILIES

The fact that fulfillment for each of us
means the end of suffering,
it doesn't mean we travel the same route
or that we end up in the same place.

There's nothing unique in suffering.
Hurt is hurt and it narrows your focus,
but there is a variety of sameness
both in suffering and fulfillment.

My bet is that fulfillment is more variegated
than suffering, suffering being narrow, fulfillment wide.

Tolstoy got it wrong on both counts:
all unhappy families are more alike
and all happy families more unalike
each other.

BREAKING A GLASS

Apart from dancing while holding aloft
the bride and groom in their chairs, for me
the most affecting part of a Jewish wedding
is when the groom breaks a glass under his heel,

reminding the couple and us that there is danger
in satisfaction, that even a temple can be destroyed and
that no one eludes menace, that there's never a good time
for smugness. A life wants to live the good and the bad

even if its person only wants what's pleasant.
A heel that beaks a glass can also break tyranny
even if living among tyrants is no one's wish
and a dangerous business.

CULTURAL DISCOVERY

Some Canadians would tell you that Fargo is for shopping
but I can tell you that Fargo is a place for cultural discovery.
For instance, Rabbi Janeen at Temple Beth El is always
worth a visit. She can realign your faith, which is better than
having your tires done – though you shouldn't forget about safety.

On this last two-day sojourn I discovered Bill Holm, a late poet
from Minnesota whose new and selected I found at Barnes & Noble.
Why did I not know this Icelandic-American poet who wrote
about real things? Now I do and I can thank Fargo for it. Not to forget
I found a beautiful pair of western boots at the RCC store in the mall.

HOARFROST

I'm sure it's nothing personal
not some sarcastic response by nature
but despite everything this January in Winnipeg
has dressed our urban forest in hoarfrost.
Tops of trees glimmer in the morning light
as if to say that during days of misery
beauty still claims its rank in the order,
that we should not forget the larger context
nor the flow of the real. If we could
only learn to read the language of things,
come to the resting place of what happens
hoarfrost in January would not surprise.

A FRIEND FROM WAY BACK WHEN

Running into a friend at an exhibition,
a friend from way back
when we thought the revolution was near
and the work we did in art important
to its advent, was a reminder
of how fine it all turned out.

We're a lot older, of course
some, many of our group, didn't get this far.
His hair is still red, mine is all grey,
silver if you want to be cultured.
He's still gaunt, I'm more like a pear,
but we both still believe.

We've learnt that ideologies suck.
That was clear from our omissions.
Human flourishing is still the goal,
no one is a means to someone's end
and there's much work left to do.
We could compare current cases.

Tacitly we were both aware
there's no shortcut on this path.
His youthful smile made me grateful
when he spoke of his efforts
on behalf of a colleague. I grew
nostalgic for the future.

THE MISERIES OF AN EARLY FALL

The miseries of an early fall have set in; high winds
downpour, speck of sun, drizzle – repeat.

But in the mall I saw not a single sour face
though it was packed with shoppers
some rushing about, from one end to the other.

Young and old lovers walked hand in hand
and teenagers sucked Slurpees,
all coffee outlets were teeming.

In this swarm of classes and colours
even the scarily decorated seemed intent
to let scrapping lie for another day.

Lots of babies were out in strollers,
all enjoying the effects of a good sale.

PALM SPRINGS

WILLIS PALMS OASIS

Do you remember us walking
along the Willis Palms Oasis that first time?

Your water bottle was hanging off your hip
the green holder bouncing to your step.

We stopped by a burnt trunk lying in the sand
next to a grove of fan palms reaching out

of the ground and us looking for
the water source and realizing it was

brought from below, pushed up
by the fault we were walking on.

Our lives shifted along with our reach,
an event we didn't realize for a while.

There under dry leafy skirts, orioles, borers,
paper wasps, spiders and lizards were hiding,

feeding on stem and fruit while we nourished
on the shaded sun and the water from your bottle.

ABOVE PALM CANYON

The West Trail climbs through Sage,
Creosote, Barrel Cacti and Cholla.

Beyond the boulders on the first rim

we take a path just evacuated by wild horses,
sweet-smelling apples steam in red sand.

ART SMITH TRAIL

A lizard may agitate sand but stillness comes back
forced by the geological pulse of ochre rocks. A mind whispers,

preserve this!

A pulse of desire intrudes on the wind from the city
and I remember: you, too, live in the noise and I yell,

preserve that also!

LAZULI BUNTING PAIR

A Lazuli Bunting pair, sleek brown female,
multi-hued, cinnamon-breasted male,
perch in the desert-olive, etching an icon
into the pale blue sky, as if intended.

Nothing could be more right
nor show a better fit with us
hiding inside, behind the blinds,
laughing and leaving things be.

LOUD SEAGULL-LIKE SCREAMS

Loud seagull-like screams approach
and the sky reveals an Osprey
gliding above the palms.

It won't find fish
in this desert; it must return across the range
or head for the Salton Sea.

It issues a challenge as it circles above us,
as if to say, "don't be surprised by surprises;
nothing is only what it seems."

THE FOLDS OF THE SAN JACINTO

A mist cloaks the folds of the San Jacinto,
conjuring the coyness of a Japanese watercolor.

Like the human brain this range of rock,
pushed up through ages of quakes
and turmoil, suspends a powerful energy
that will, one day, demand release.

TAHQUITZ CANYON CREEK

A dry creek bed
during the hottest part of the day
when radiation shimmers off the levee
stones and even the tumbleweed won't
move a thought. If you're lucky
you may find a tiny puddle under the bridge
its dark water impurely reflecting the world.

Dogs off leash sniff through the area
and do what they must. Their master trails
far behind, his every step approached
as an assignment. Only the Moon Flowers,
the Smokethorns and the Flycatchers seem content
as if they knew that this too will pass all too soon.

THE McCALLUM GROVE

The pond is clear, it's whitish sand embellished
with broken bits of blackening palm. Desert Pupfish
and bullfrog tadpoles scatter in a dance among the reeds
when you approach. Tall palms guard this pond as if the face
you spot leaning in over its surface were a treasure.

The San Andreas Fault created this oasis, this view
of yourself – and once you've seen it, you can walk
over to the dune and scout for another rarity:
the Coachella Valley fringe-toed lizard. But do linger
for this lizard less happily reveals its shovel-shaped face
and you may have to content yourself with spotting its tracks
the parallel lines of lattice in the sand,
falling victim to an indifferent wind.

A THEORY OF RELATIVITY

The mouse sitting under the Paloverde
demonstrates its superior perspective:
by being closer to the ground she has
the truer feel of desert sands. Undoubtedly
she could address discrepancies among grains.

The Red-tailed Hawk though reads patterns.
The mouse is innocent of such wider contexts
so she won't notice that it is she who teaches
the hawk how to touch the ground.

STILL WAVES

The still waves of the San Jacinto range
can settle your heart if you let them.

They know of beginning's brutal roiling
and of how to sit tight and enjoy the wait.

They are sentinels separating the valley where seraphim slept
and the lights of dream city. Of course, they tremble,

but they endure and stay true to task
keeping the desert away from the coast.

THE L.A. FREEWAY SYSTEM

Driving at 80 mph on the L.A. freeway system
(in spurts because for long periods we're down to 30
or we seem parked) gives the illusion of purpose
in a day crowded with chaos. Here everyone on our side
of the road is headed in the same direction – or should be –
even though our destinations are different.

If life's purpose were so simply designed
that we traveled in the same direction as everyone else
in our lane, imagine how boring that would be?
(This may explain a lot of the recklessness on the freeways).
Thankfully life allows each of us our own direction yet it gets us all
to the same place.

SPLOTCHES

There are splotches of clouds floating
like someone had flung huge pieces of washboard into the sky
and the mountains are getting darker as the sun sets behind them.
Someone is reading Proverbs to steel his soul
against the coming of night
while three Snowy Egrets seek a place to sleep
"what you fear you will find," Solomon warned.

A STRIP MALL

There's a strip mall right up against the mountains.
You can get an adjustable bed there and a 99 cent Whopper
among other things.
The parking lot is decorated
with California Fan Palms and Canary Island Date Palms.
The buildings are in earth tones and the whole thing
is a lot less offensive to the eye
than you'd expect,
up against the grayish-brown hills
long ago vacated by Bighorn Sheep.

MURRAY CANYON

Walking into Murray Canyon today
is like entering creation's workshop.
After the rains the mountains are green with weeds
and Fountain Grass stand in healthy clusters along the trail.
New palm fronds shoot from the ground along the creek
that rushes louder and more clearly than it has in months.
The Sage wears a deeper silvery green and sports yellow flowers.
Honey Mesquites whose branches were barren a short while ago
have sprouted new leaflets.

At the end of the trail by the Seven Sisters waterfall
a Desert Iguana draws a delighted taunt from a little boy
singing to his older brother, "I saw an Iguana and
you-oo didn't!" bringing us back to our present concerns
by reminding us that beauty is not enough.
Curiosity and playful competition spurs a human ecology
where the young are allowed the loudest laughs.

JOY

When I envision joy
I see you and me dancing
on the desert floor, the sun
hanging above the mountains
the moon pregnant in the blue eastern sky.
I see cacti and ancient creosote,
drinking our rhythms
and I hear your gasps
it is good, it is good, it is all good,
while a hawk and his mate glide
in the updraft we've created.

JOSHUA TREE PARK

Boredom's contempt for ordinary realities
drove us into Joshua Tree Park today
looking for a challenge on the Ryan Mountain trail
for which we were rewarded by a sight of the beauty
that stretches far into Mexico.
Having made the hike before we saw again that repetition
brings its own blessings,
that no trail is ever the same from one day to the next
even as you tread on the same rock
and that they all end in unexpected views.
You may have seen before, though never again like this.

NO DOGS ALLOWED

Endangered Peninsular bighorn sheep are lambing
and trails have been closed to dog walkers.
Signs screaming NO DOGS ALLOWED BEYOND THIS POINT
have been torn down on the trail
leading into the Magnesia Springs Preserve
from the end of Desert Drive in Rancho Mirage
where the most common cars spotted are Lexus, Benz and BMW.
As one dog owner states, "it's hard because my dog has nowhere else
to exercise," and what could be more important, you might ask.
In the lambing season the bighorn sheep are used to fighting
mountain lions, coyotes and wild dogs
who find the scent of birth and young blood irresistible.
It is their nature, after all.
Now they also have to fight people walking the dog,
because privilege will not tolerate inconvenience,
naturally.

READ ALL ABOUT IT

You can read all about it in the sky
and in the canyons or in braided palm trunks
not to mention in the talons of a hawk,
a raven's beak.
You can also read snowy peaks and the water
that fills creeks in winter months
and the tracks roadrunners leave in moist sand.
There are metaphoric rocks and magnesia-filled boulders
holding on to fables that cannot be unraveled without violence
and footprints all over the valley left by city planners
trying to contain a sprawling story.
But if you can read between lines
check out the tales among the lizard prints
and you'll find that this is truly some god's country.

ABOUT PER K. BRASK

Per K. Brask is an accomplished dramaturge and author, with published poetry, plays, short stories, essays and literary translations. *A Spectator*, his first collection of ekphrastic poetry, was published in 2012. He lives in Winnipeg, Canada, with his wife, Carol Matas, an award-winning young-adult fiction author. He teaches in the Department of Theatre and Film at the University of Winnipeg.

For a more complete biography, visit: fictivepress.com/per-brask.htm.

www.ingramcontent.com/pod-product-compliance
Lightning Source LLC
Chambersburg PA
CBHW031226090426
42740CB00007B/730